Huskyology Trivia Challenge

UConn Huskies Basketball

Huskyology Trivia Challenge

UConn Huskies Basketball

Researched by Paul F. Wilson

Paul F. Wilson & Tom P. Rippey III, Editors

Kick The Ball, Ltd
Lewis Center, Ohio

Trivia by Kick The Ball, Ltd

College Football Trivia

Alabama Crimson Tide	Auburn Tigers	Boston College Eagles	Florida Gators
Georgia Bulldogs	LSU Tigers	Miami Hurricanes	Michigan Wolverines
Nebraska Cornhuskers	Notre Dame Fighting Irish	Ohio State Buckeyes	Oklahoma Sooners
Oregon Ducks	Penn State Nittany Lions	Southern Cal Trojans	Texas Longhorns

Pro Football Trivia

Arizona Cardinals	Buffalo Bills	Chicago Bears	Cleveland Browns
Denver Broncos	Green Bay Packers	Indianapolis Colts	Kansas City Chiefs
Minnesota Vikings	New England Patriots	Oakland Raiders	Pittsburgh Steelers
San Francisco 49ers	Washington Redskins		

Pro Baseball Trivia

Boston Red Sox	Chicago Cubs	Cincinnati Reds	Los Angeles Dodgers
New York Yankees	Philadelphia Phillies	Saint Louis Cardinals	

College Basketball Trivia

Duke Blue Devils	Georgetown Hoyas	Indiana Hoosiers	Kansas Jayhawks
Kentucky Wildcats	Maryland Terrapins	Michigan State Spartans	North Carolina Tar Heels
Syracuse Orange	UConn Huskies	UCLA Bruins	

Pro Basketball Trivia

Boston Celtics	Chicago Bulls	Detroit Pistons	Los Angeles Lakers
Utah Jazz			

Visit **www.TriviaGameBooks.com** for more details.

This book is dedicated to our families and friends for your unwavering love, support, and your understanding of our pursuit of our passions. Thank you for everything you do for us and for making our lives complete.

Huskyology Trivia Challenge – UConn Huskies Basketball;
First Edition 2009

Published by
Kick The Ball, Ltd
8595 Columbus Pike, Suite 197
Lewis Center, OH 43035
www.TriviaGameBooks.com

Designed, Formatted, and Edited by: Paul F. Wilson & Tom P. Rippey III
Researched by: Paul F. Wilson

*For information on ordering this book in bulk at reduced prices, please email us
at pfwilson@triviagamebooks.com.*

International Standard Book Number: 978-1-934372-74-6

Printed and Bound in the United States of America

10 9 8 7 6 5 4 3 2 1

Table of Contents

Dear Friend,

Thank you for purchasing our *Huskyology Trivia Challenge* game book!

We have made every attempt to verify the accuracy of the questions and answers contained in this book. However it is still possible that from time to time an error has been made by us or our researchers. In the event you find a question or answer that is questionable or inaccurate, we ask for your understanding and thank you for bringing it to our attention so we may improve future editions of this book. Please email us at tprippey@triviagamebooks.com with those observations and comments.

Have fun playing *Huskyology Trivia Challenge*!

Paul & Tom

Paul Wilson & Tom Rippey
Co-Founders, Kick The Ball, Ltd

PS – You can discover more about all of our current trivia game books by visiting www.TriviaGameBooks.com.

Book Format:

There are four quarters, each made up of fifty questions. Each quarter's questions have assigned point values. Questions are designed to get progressively more difficult as you proceed through each quarter, as well as through the book itself. Most questions are in a four-option multiple-choice format so that you will at least have a 25% chance of getting a correct answer for some of the more challenging questions.

We have even added an overtime section in the event of a tie, or just in case you want to keep playing a little longer.

Game Options:

One Player -
To play on your own, simply answer each of the questions in all the quarters, and in the overtime section, if you'd like. Use the Player / Team Score Sheet to record your answers and the quarter Answer Keys to check your answers. Calculate each quarter's points and the total for the game at the bottom of the Player / Team Score Sheet to determine your final score.

Two or More Players –
To play with multiple players decide if you will all be competing with each other individually, or if you will form and play as teams. Each player / team will then have its own Player / Team Score Sheet to record its answer. You can use the quarter Answer Keys to check your answers and to calculate your final scores.

The Player / Team Score Sheets have been designed so that each team can answer all questions or you can divide the questions up in any combination you would prefer. For example, you may want to alternate questions if two players are playing or answer every third question for three players, etc. In any case, simply record your response to your questions in the corresponding quarter and question number on the Player / Team Score Sheet.

A winner will be determined by multiplying the total number of correct answers for each quarter by the point value per quarter, then adding together the final total for all quarters combined. Play the game again and again by alternating the questions that your team is assigned so that you will answer a different set of questions each time you play.

You Create the Game -
There are countless other ways of using *Huskyology Trivia Challenge* questions. It is limited only to your imagination. Examples might be using them at your tailgate or other college basketball related party. Players / Teams who answer questions incorrectly may have to perform a required action, or winners may receive special prizes. Let us know what other games you come up with!

Have fun!

1) What year did the nickname Huskies become widely associated with the University of Connecticut?

Answers begin on page 17

    A) 1930
    B) 1934
    C) 1940
    D) 1944

2) What are the Huskies' official colors?

    A) White and Gray
    B) Gray and Blue
    C) Blue and White
    D) Blue and Black

3) What is the name of UConn's home arena?

    A) UC Husky Dome
    B) Mark R. Shenkman Center
    C) The Burton Family Complex
    D) Harry A. Gampel Pavilion

4) How many Naismith College Player of the Year winners played at UConn?

    A) 0
    B) 1
    C) 2
    D) 3

5) What is the official name of UConn's fight song?

    A)   "Fight On Huskies"
    B)   "Husky Fight"
    C)   "UConn Husky"
    D)   "Husky Pride"

6) How many Huskies have won an Olympic gold medal for basketball?

    A) 0
    B) 1
    C) 4
    D) 7

7) How many times has UConn appeared in the NCAA Final Four?

    A) 0
    B) 1
    C) 2
    D) 3

8) Who has the longest coaching tenure at UConn?

    A)   Jim Calhoun
    B)   Dominic Perno
    C)   Hugh Greer
    D)   Don White

9) What year did UConn join the Big East?

- A) 1959
- B) 1969
- C) 1979
- D) 1989

10) What season was UConn's first-ever overtime game?

- A) 1948-49
- B) 1956-57
- C) 1963-64
- D) 1970-71

11) Who led the Huskies in total rebounds in the 2008-09 season?

- A) A.J. Price
- B) Stanley Robinson
- C) Jeff Adrien
- D) Hasheem Thabeet

12) Gampel Pavilion's seating capacity for UConn basketball is over 10,000.

- A) True
- B) False

13) What is the name of UConn's live mascot?

    A) Jesse
    B) James
    C) Jeffrey
    D) Jonathan

14) Which company is UConn's exclusive partner for footwear, apparel, and equipment?

    A) Reebok
    B) Adidas
    C) Nike
    D) Converse

15) Which Big East opponent has UConn played the most number of times in its history?

    A) Villanova
    B) Georgetown
    C) Providence
    D) Syracuse

16) What season did the Huskies play their first-ever game?

    A) 1900-01
    B) 1904-05
    C) 1907-08
    D) 1911-12

17) Did UConn score greater than 3,000 points as a team in the 2008-09 season?

   A) Yes
   B) No

18) What arena is UConn's home away from home?

   A) XL Center
   B) Excel Center
   C) LX Center
   D) CH Center

19) In what country was UConn standout Hasheem Thabeet born?

   A) Trinidad & Tobago
   B) Tunisia
   C) Tuvalu
   D) Tanzania

20) Who was the first consensus First Team All-American at UConn?

   A) Richard Hamilton
   B) Ray Allen
   C) Donyell Marshall
   D) Hasheem Thabeet

21) Did UConn have a winning record their first-ever season?

    A) Yes
    B) No

22) What nickname was given to the 1990 UConn basketball season?

    A) Legendary
    B) Destiny
    C) Dream Season
    D) Redemption

23) Which UConn head coach has the most all-time career wins?

    A) Hugh Greer
    B) Dominic Perno
    C) Donald Rowe
    D) Jim Calhoun

24) Which of the following Huskies only received one NCAA All-Tournament selection?

    A) Ricky Moore
    B) Richard Hamilton
    C) Khalid El-Amin
    D) Emeka Okafor

25) Who holds UConn's all-time record for most assists in a single game?

    A) Craig Austrie
    B) Kevin Ollie
    C) Earl Kelley
    D) Marcus Williams

26) When was UConn's first-ever undefeated season (minimum 10 games)?

    A) 1913
    B) 1956
    C) 1983
    D) None of the above

27) What is UConn's team record for most consecutive NCAA Tournament appearances?

    A) 2
    B) 3
    C) 5
    D) 7

28) The Huskies had two two-loss seasons under Coach Calhoun.

    A) True
    B) False

29) How many consecutive seasons did UConn not have a coach in the early 1900s?

A) 5
B) 10
C) 15
D) 20

30) How many games did UConn play in St. Thomas, U.S. Virgin Islands in 2008-09?

A) 0
B) 1
C) 2
D) 3

31) What term is used to characterize enthusiasm for UConn basketball?

A) Huskydom
B) Huskymania
C) Husky Madness
D) Husky Mayhem

32) How many overtime games did UConn play in 2008-09?

A) 1
B) 2
C) 3
D) 4

33) How many seasons in school history have the Huskies gone undefeated at home?

A) 0
B) 2
C) 5
D) 8

34) Where did assistant head coach George Blaney coach immediate before joining UConn?

A) Holy Cross
B) Seton Hall
C) Georgetown
D) Providence

35) Who was the only team to score greater than 90 points against UConn in the 2008-09 regular season?

A) Syracuse
B) Pittsburgh
C) Michigan State
D) None of the above

36) How many games did the NCAA force UConn to vacate in 1996?

A) 1
B) 2
C) 3
D) 4

37) Which player holds the record for most points scored in a single game against UConn?

    A)   Ronnie Perry, Holy Cross
    B)   Al Butler, Niagara
    C)   Jack Foley, Holy Cross
    D)   Darius Rice, Miami

38) UConn has more Big East Tournament titles than Louisville, Providence, and Villanova combined.

    A)   True
    B)   False

39) What is the name of the all-male a cappella ensemble that can be heard performing the National Anthem at Huskies games?

    A)   UConn Men's Choral
    B)   Conn-men
    C)   Husky Pride Singers
    D)   There is no such group

40) What offense does Jim Calhoun employ at UConn?

    A)   Triangle Offense
    B)   1-3-1 Cutters Offense
    C)   3-Out 2-In Motion Offense
    D)   Dribble Drive Motion Offense

41) How many all-time NCAA National Championships has UConn won?

A) 1
B) 2
C) 3
D) 5

42) Since 1900, how many seasons has UConn not played basketball?

A) 3
B) 5
C) 7
D) None of the above

43) Who was the Huskies' first-ever opponent at Gampel Pavilion?

A) Boston College
B) Fairfield
C) St. John's
D) Providence

44) In the 2008-09 season, did UConn go undefeated at home in conference play?

A) Yes
B) No

45) Who holds UConn's record for career blocks?

    A) Hasheem Thabeet
    B) Donyell Marshall
    C) Josh Boone
    D) Emeka Okafor

46) UConn's Hasheem Thabeet was named First Team All-American by what organization in 2009?

    A) *The Sporting News*
    B) Associated Press
    C) National Association of Basketball Coaches
    D) United States Basketball Writers Association

47) What are the most losses in a season by UConn at home?

    A) 9
    B) 11
    C) 13
    D) 15

48) Who holds UConn's record for most points scored in a single game?

    A) Wes Bialosuknia
    B) Bill Corley
    C) Art Quimby
    D) Toby Kimball

49) UConn's Ray Allen was drafted by the Minnesota Timberwolves in 1996.

    A) Yes
    B) No

50) What season did UConn celebrate its first-ever victory over Syracuse?

    A) 1955-56
    B) 1958-59
    C) 1959-60
    D) 1962-63

The University of Connecticut is fortunate to have two highly accomplished basketball teams on campus. Both the women's and men's squads have achieved national prominence in recent years. Since polls play an important part in ranking college teams during the regular season, it is interesting to note that only two NCAA Division 1 programs, Connecticut and Duke, have ever had both their women's and men's basketball teams earn no.1 rankings at the same time in the AP Poll. In fact, the Huskies have accomplished this feat an unprecedented three times. On Feb. 13, 1995, Nov. 30, 1998, and from preseason to Nov. 25, 2003 both the lady Huskies and Huskies were ranked No. 1 in the AP Poll. With such low probably of occurrence, this is one hat trick UConn can be exceptionally proud of.

1) B – 1934 (The Husky was chosen as the school mascot in 1934 following a 1933 school name change to Connecticut State College.)

2) C – Blue and White (School colors since the mid-1890s; In 1952 National Flag Blue [navy] was designated as the color standard for athletic logos by school trustees.)

3) D – Harry A. Gampel Pavilion (The pavilion is the Storrs, Conn. home of UConn's men's and women's basketball.)

4) A – 0 (Through the 2008-09 season no Huskies have been given this honor.)

5) C – "UConn Husky" (Written by Herbert France in the 1940s)

6) B – 1 (Ray Allen was a member of the gold-medal-winning 2000 Olympic USA Men's Basketball Team.)

7) D – 3 (1998-99, 2003-04, and 2008-09)

8) A – Jim Calhoun (Coach Calhoun is entering his 23rd season as UConn men's basketball head coach in 2009-10.)

9) C – 1979 (UConn was a founding member of the Big East along with Boston College, Georgetown, Providence, Seton Hall, St. John's, and Syracuse.)

10) B – 1956-57 (On Dec. 29, 1956, UConn played into its first recorded overtime versus Pittsburgh. UConn would go on to win that game 64-50.)

11) D – Hasheem Thabeet (Thabeet corralled 388 total rebounds [133 OFF and 255 DEF] in 2008-09.)

12) A – True (Seating capacity is 10,167 since 2002.)

13) D – Jonathan (The name was selected in a contest in 1935. The mascot's namesake is Jonathon Trumbull, Connecticut's Governor during the Revolutionary War.)

14) C – Nike (As part of the $45.5 million 10-year agreement, Nike is contributing $1 million to the construction of the new UConn basketball practice facility.)

15) D – Syracuse (The Huskies and the Orange have faced off 83 times in the regular season since 1956.)

16) A – 1900-01 (UConn played Windham High in their first-ever game.)

17) B – No (2,819 total team points for the season)

18) A – XL Center (The XL Center is UConn's second home, located in Hartford, Conn.)

19) D – Tanzania (Dar es Salaam, Tanzania on Feb. 16, 1987)

20) C – Donyell Marshall (25.1 points per game, 302 total rebounds, 111 blocked shots in 1993-94)

21) A – Yes (UConn was 1-0 their first-ever recorded season of men's basketball [1900-01].)

22) C – Dream Season (The preseason unranked Huskies would go on to win the Big East Regular Season and Tournament Championships in their first season playing at Gampel Pavilion.)

23) D – Jim Calhoun (Coach Calhoun has amassed 553 career wins at UConn.)

24) A – Ricky Moore (Ricky's only selection was in 1999. Hamilton and El-Amin were selected in 1998 and 1999. Emeka Okafor was selected in 2003 and 2004.)

25) D – Marcus Williams (Marcus had 16 assists in a game twice. The most recent was versus Notre Dame on Jan. 30, 2005. His first was on Dec. 22, 2004 versus CCSU.)

26) D – None of the above (UConn has never had an undefeated season, in seasons with more than one game played.)

27) C – 5 (The Huskies have had two separate streaks of five appearances in a row, 1956-60 and 2002-06.)

28) A – True (1995-96 [30-2] and 1998-99 [34-2])

29) C – 15 (The team had no official head coach from 1900-15.)

30) D – 3 (The Huskies were 3-0 in the 2008-09 season's Paradise Jam tournament.)

31) B – Huskymania (One way UConn students and supporters demonstrate Huskymania is during their rhythmic clapping while standing during games.)

32) A – 1 (The six-overtime game versus Syracuse Orange on March 12, 2009, became an instant Big East classic [UConn 117, Syracuse 127].)

33) C – 5 (1953-54 [11-0], 1993-94 [15-0], 1995-96 [15-0], 1997-98 [17-0], and 2005-06 [16-0])

34) B – Seton Hall (Blaney was head coach of Seton Hall for three years prior to joining Jim Calhoun on the bench at UConn. Prior to Seton Hall he was head coach of Holy Cross for 22 years.)

35) D – None of the above (No team scored 90 or more points against the Huskies in the 2008-09 regular season.)

36) C – 3 (UConn's 1996 NCAA Tournament games were nullified by action of the NCAA.)

37) D – Jack Foley, Holy Cross (Jack "The Shot" Foley lit up the nets for 56 points against UConn on Feb. 17, 1962 [UConn 64, Holy Cross 103].)

38) A – True (Connecticut has won six titles [1990, 1996, 1998, 1999, 2002, and 2004]. Louisville [2009], Providence [1994], and Villanova [1995] have only combined for three.)

39) B – Conn-men (The group was formed in 2001, with a repertoire including The UConn Alma Mater and the National Anthem among others.)

40) C – 3-Out 2-In Motion Offense (Coach Calhoun even developed an instructional video about his offense called "Jim Calhoun: The Attacking 3-Out 2-In Motion Offense".)

41) B – 2 (UConn won the NCAA National Championship in 1999 and 2004.)

42) A – 3 (1908-09, 1909-10, and 1913-14)

43) C – St. John's (The Huskies played their first-ever game at Gampel Pavilion on Jan. 27, 1990, a game they won 72-58 in front of 8,241 fans.)

44) B – No (UConn lost to both Georgetown [74-63] and Pittsburgh [76-68] at XL Center in 2008-09.)

45) D – Emeka Okafor (441 career blocked shots from 2002-04)

46) C – National Association of Basketball Coaches (The NABC was the only major organization giving him the honor.)

47) A – 9 (In 1986-87 the Huskies were 7-9 at home. Note: Win-loss records broken out by home and away are not available for seasons 1848-49 and earlier.)

48) B – Bill Corley (Bill scored 51 points versus New Hampshire on Jan. 10, 1968 [UConn 96, New Hampshire 70].)

49) A – Yes (Allen was selected with the 5th overall pick by the Timberwolves in the 1996 NBA Draft.)

50) D – 1962-63 (UConn did not defeat Syracuse in their first seven meetings. It was not until March 7, 1963, that UConn would beat the Orange [UConn 92, Syracuse 74].)

Note: All answers valid as of the end of the 2008-09 season, unless otherwise indicated in the question itself.

1) How many times has UConn won by 70 or more points?

Answers begin on page 37

   A) 0
   B) 1
   C) 3
   D) 5

2) Which UConn player led the team in assists in the 2008-09 season?

   A) Kemba Walker
   B) Craig Austrie
   C) Jerome Dyson
   D) A.J. Price

3) Which UConn head coach had the second longest tenure?

   A) Donald Rowe
   B) Dominic Perno
   C) Hugh Greer
   D) Don White

4) How many decades has UConn won at least 200 games?

   A) 1
   B) 2
   C) 5
   D) 6

5) What was the name of the first athletic conference to which UConn belonged?

    A)   Colonial Athletic Association
    B)   Atlantic Ten Conference
    C)   Yankee Conference
    D)   East Coast Conference

6) Has UConn ever played 40 or more games in a single season?

    A) Yes
    B) No

7) Which player holds the record for most rebounds against UConn in a single Big East game?

    A)   Michael Smith
    B)   Jerome Lane
    C)   Patrick Ewing
    D)   Dikembe Mutombo

8) Since 1980, what are the fewest points the Huskies have scored in a half?

    A) 5
    B) 9
    C) 14
    D) 18

9) What is UConn's team record for most games won by a four-year senior class?

    A) 94
    B) 104
    C) 114
    D) 124

10) Has UConn ever lost to any of the U.S. Service Academies?

    A) Yes
    B) No

11) What is UConn's all-time winning percentage against Seton Hall?

    A) .390
    B) .490
    C) .590
    D) .690

12) Which current non-conference opponent has UConn played the most number of times?

    A) UMass
    B) Maine
    C) Rhode Island
    D) New Hampshire

13) How many times has UConn played in a triple-overtime regular-season game?

    A) 2
    B) 4
    C) 6
    D) 8

14) Who holds UConn's career record for most points scored?

    A) Richard Hamilton
    B) Chris Smith
    C) Tony Hanson
    D) Ray Allen

15) What is UConn's single-game record for most steals as a team?

    A) 13
    B) 19
    C) 24
    D) 28

16) Which team handed UConn its worst loss ever?

    A) St. Bonaventure
    B) Holly Cross
    C) Sacred Heart
    D) Wesleyan

17) What are the most consecutive NCAA Tournaments to which Jim Calhoun has coached UConn?

   A) 2
   B) 3
   C) 5
   D) 7

18) In the 2008-09 season, what were the fewest points UConn allowed in a single game (including tournaments)?

   A) 47
   B) 49
   C) 50
   D) 51

19) What is UConn's longest winning streak in the UConn-Syracuse series?

   A) 3 games
   B) 4 games
   C) 7 games
   D) 8 games

20) Have the Huskies won 50 or more NCAA Tournament games?

   A) Yes
   B) No

21) Who is the only UConn player to win Big East Player of the Year more than once?

    A)   Richard Hamilton
    B)   Donyell Marshall
    C)   Emeka Okafor
    D)   None of the above

22) From 1995 to 2009 how many weeks has UConn been ranked No. 1 in the AP Poll?

    A)   16
    B)   19
    C)   25
    D)   28

23) Which UConn Husky was the most recent recipient of the Big East Rookie of the Year Award?

    A)   Khalid El-Amin
    B)   Doron Sheffer
    C)   Rudy Gay
    D)   Nadav Henefeld

24) How many times has UConn played North Carolina in the NCAA Tournament?

    A)   0
    B)   1
    C)   2
    D)   3

25) Which UConn head coach has the second most all-time career wins?

    A) Dominic Perno
    B) Don White
    C) Hugh Greer
    D) Donald Rowe

26) Did the Huskies have a game in the 2008-09 season in which they scored fewer than 50 points?

    A) Yes
    B) No

27) Which opponent has UConn played the most in the Big East Tournament Championship game?

    A) Syracuse
    B) Pittsburgh
    C) Georgetown
    D) Seton Hall

28) What is UConn's individual record for most rebounds in a single game?

    A) 22
    B) 28
    C) 34
    D) 40

29) All time, how many of UConn's games have gone into overtime (regular season and tournament)?

 A) 59
 B) 69
 C) 79
 D) 89

30) What is UConn's record for consecutive winning seasons?

 A) 16
 B) 18
 C) 20
 D) 22

31) Who was UConn's first-ever NCAA Tournament opponent?

 A) St. John's
 B) Navy
 C) Manhattan
 D) Temple

32) How many times have UConn players won Big East Player of the Year?

 A) 3
 B) 5
 C) 7
 D) 8

33) What is UConn's team record for most three-pointers made in a single game?

A) 9
B) 10
C) 14
D) 15

34) How many times has UConn played in the postseason NIT Tournament?

A) 9
B) 11
C) 13
D) 15

35) How many points was UConn's largest-ever loss to Syracuse?

A) 40
B) 44
C) 48
D) 52

36) Have the Huskies ever gone from being ranked No. 1 in the Preseason AP Poll to not ranked No. 1 for the rest of the season?

A) Yes
B) No

37) Who led the Huskies in free-throw percentage in the 2008-09 season (minimum 50 attempts)?

    A)   Kemba Walker
    B)   Jerome Dyson
    C)   A.J. Price
    D)   Craig Austrie

38) How many times have UConn players been named to the All-NCAA Final Four Team?

    A)   4
    B)   6
    C)   8
    D)   10

39) Who holds UConn's record for steals in a season?

    A)   Nadav Henefeld
    B)   Bobby Dulin
    C)   Scott Burrell
    D)   Doron Sheffer

40) Which season did the Huskies first record 20 wins?

    A)   1915-16
    B)   1938-39
    C)   1950-51
    D)   1964-65

41) Against which Big East Conference opponent does UConn have the most all-time wins?

   A) Pittsburgh
   B) Syracuse
   C) Seton Hall
   D) Providence

42) Which team did UConn not play in the 2009 NCAA Tournament?

   A) Michigan State
   B) Purdue
   C) Gonzaga
   D) Missouri

43) Who holds UConn's record for most games played in a career?

   A) Kevin Freeman
   B) Ricky Moore
   C) Denham Brown
   D) Jake Voskuhl

44) What are the most consecutive Big East Regular-Season Championships the Huskies have won?

   A) 2
   B) 3
   C) 5
   D) 6

45) Has a UConn player ever led the nation in scoring?

   A) Yes
   B) No

46) What is UConn's all-time consecutive home wins record?

   A) 24 games
   B) 27 games
   C) 31 games
   D) 35 games

47) In the 2008-09 season, how many UConn players averaged 10 or more points per game?

   A) 3
   B) 4
   C) 6
   D) 7

48) Which current non-conference opponent has the most all-time wins against UConn?

   A) Boston College
   B) Maine
   C) New Hampshire
   D) Yale

49) What year did UConn win its first-ever regular-season Big East Championship?

    A) 1980
    B) 1983
    C) 1986
    D) 1990

50) Who was UConn's opponent when they appeared in the Jimmy V Classic?

    A) Davidson
    B) USC
    C) Memphis
    D) None of the above

Lead the league for one year and you will get noticed. Lead it for two years in a row, and you will get much deserved respect. Now jump ahead, way ahead and lead it for eight straight years and you are a bona fide juggernaut. That is exactly the type of sheer dominance the Huskies have when it comes to blocking shots in the league. Since 2002 the Huskies have led the NCAA Division 1 ranks by blocking the most shots per game each season. No other team has ever exerted such control in this statistical category. UConn does it with tenacious play and outstanding rhythm and timing on the defensive end of the court. Whether an opponent is shooting from the perimeter or driving to the basket, they know the kings of swat await them.

1) B – 1 (UConn defeated CCSU 116-46 on Dec. 20, 1969.)

2) D – A.J. Price (Price had 164 assists throughout the 2008-09 season.)

3) C – Hugh Greer (Coach Greer led UConn for 17 seasons from 1946-63.)

4) B – 2 (1990s [224 wins] and 2000s [224 wins and counting])

5) C – Yankee Conference (A Division 1 Conference, the Yankee Conference became defunct in 1997.)

6) B – No (The most games the Huskies have played in a single season is 39 [2003-04].)

7) D – Dikembe Mutombo (Mutombo gathered 27 boards versus UConn on March 8, 1991, in the Big East Tournament in Madison Square Garden [UConn 49, Georgetown 68].)

8) B – 9 (On Dec. 10, 2002, UConn was held to nine points in a half by UMass. Despite the low production in that half, the Huskies won the game 59-48.)

9) C – 114 (Ricky Moore, Rashamel Jones, and Antric Klaiber had a class record of 114-24 by their 1998-99 senior year.)

10) A – Yes (UConn is 2-0 vs. Air Force, 7-3 vs. Army, 24-9 vs. Coast Guard, and 0-1 vs. Navy.)

11) D – .690 (The Huskies enjoy a 40-18 all-time record versus the Pirates.)

12) C – Rhode Island (UConn has met RI in 145 basketball games throughout the years. From 1906-2000 UConn is 77-68 [.531] versus RI.)

13) A – 2 (Rhode Island with a 70-80 loss on Feb. 5, 1974 and Syracuse with an 85-87 loss on Feb. 18, 1984)

14) B – Chris Smith (From 1989-92 Chris scored 2,145 career points.)

15) C – 24 (On Dec. 7, 1989, UConn stole the ball 24 times to set a school record vs. Hartford [UConn 79, Hartford 54].)

16) D – Wesleyan (In the 1905-06 season Wesleyan defeated UConn 86-12 [74 point margin of victory].)

17) C – 5 (A Coach Calhoun-led Huskies team appeared in five-straight NCAA Tournaments from 2001-02 to 2005-06.)

18) A – 47 (In the first round of the NCAA Tournament UConn defeated Chattanooga 103-47.)

19) B – 4 games (From Jan. 23, 1995 to March 8, 1996, the Huskies won 4-consecutive games against the Orange.)

20) B – No (UConn has played 69 total games in the NCAA Tournament in its history with a 43-29 all-time record. Note: This includes NCAA vacated games.)

21) A – Richard Hamilton (Hamilton won the award for his outstanding play in both 1997-98 and 1998-99. He shared the honor with Miami's Tim James in 1998-99.)

22) D – 28 (This includes four weeks at No. 1 in 2008-09.)

23) C – Rudy Gay (Rudy received the award in 2004-05.)

24) B – 1 (On March 21, 1998 the Huskies played the Tar Heels in Greensboro, N.C. [UConn 64, North Carolina 75].)

25) C – Hugh Greer (Coach Greer led the Huskies to 286 victories from 1946-63.)

26) B – No (The fewest points scored by UConn in a single game in 2008-09 were 61 [61-55] versus West Virginia on Jan. 6, 2009.)

27) A – Syracuse (UConn is 5-7 versus Syracuse in the Big East Tournament Championship.)

28) D – 40 (Art Quimby grabbed 40 rebounds versus Boston College on Jan. 11, 1955, to set this long-standing UConn record.)

29) C – 79 (The most recent was the 6OT game vs. Syracuse on March 12, 2009, in which UConn lost 117-127.)

30) D – 22 (From 1987-88 through 2008-09 UConn has had 22 consecutive winning seasons.)

31) A – St. John's (UConn lost to St. John's 52-63 in New York, N.Y. on March 20, 1951, in the NCAA Tournament.)

32) C – 7 (Donyell Marshall [1993-94], Ray Allen [1995-96], Richard Hamilton [1997-98 and 1998-99], Caron Butler [2001-02], Emeka Okafor [2003-04], and Hasheem Thabeet [2008-09])

33) D – 15 (This happened in a game versus Hartford on Dec. 28, 1997 [UConn 100, Hartford 69].)

34) B – 11 (In its eleven NIT appearances UConn is 14-10. The most recent appearance took place in 2000-01.)

35) A – 40 (UConn's offense sputtered in a 61-101 loss to the Orange on Nov. 30, 1977.)

36) A – Yes (UConn is one of 7 teams in NCAA history to be ranked No. 1 in the preseason without earning a 2nd No.1 ranking through the rest of the season.)

37) D – Craig Austrie (Austrie's 72-89 [.809] shooting from the line placed him ahead of all his Husky teammates in the category.)

38) B – 6 (1999 [Richard Hamilton, Khalid El-Amin, and Ricky Moore] and 2004 [Emeka Okafor, Ben Gordon, and Rashad Anderson])

39) A – Nadav Henefeld (138 steals; 37 games in 1989-90)

40) C – 1950-51 (Coach Greer led the Huskies to a 22-4 [.846] record that season.)

41) D – Providence (UConn has a 41-26 all-time record versus the Friars.)

42) C – Gonzaga (UConn's NCAA Tournament opponents in 2009 were Chattanooga, Texas A&M, Purdue, Missouri, and Michigan State.)

43) A – Kevin Freeman (140 games from 1997-2000)

44) B – 3 (1994, 1995, and 1996)

45) B – No (Through the 2008-09 season no Husky has ever had the highest scoring average in Division 1 men's basketball.)

46) C – 31 games (The streak occurred from 2004-07.)

47) B – 4 (A.J. Price [14.7], Jeff Adrien [13.6], Hasheem Thabeet [13.6], and Jerome Dyson [13.2])

48) C – New Hampshire (NH has an 89-25 all-time record versus UConn for a .781 winning percentage.)

49) D – 1990 (31-6 overall and 12-4 Big East records helped the Huskies become Co-Champions of the Big East in 1989-90.)

50) D – None of the above (UConn has never played in the Jimmy V Men's Basketball Classic Tournament.)

Note: All answers valid as of the end of the 2008-09 season, unless otherwise indicated in the question itself.

Huskyology Trivia Challenge

1) How many times has UConn appeared in the Big East Tournament Championship game?

Answers begin on page 56

    A) 7
    B) 8
    C) 9
    D) 10

2) Who holds UConn's record for free throws made in a single Big East game?

    A) Donyell Marshall
    B) Caron Butler
    C) Richard Hamilton
    D) Cliff Robinson

3) Which season did the Huskies first record 30 wins?

    A) 1978-79
    B) 1980-81
    C) 1987-88
    D) 1989-90

4) Did any Husky have greater than fifty steals in 2008-09?

    A) Yes
    B) No

5) Which Husky player had 67 consecutive games scoring in double figures in his career?

    A)   Caron Butler
    B)   Tony Hanson
    C)   Ray Allen
    D)   Richard Hamilton

6) What is the highest jersey number ever worn by a UConn Husky?

    A)   #55
    B)   #66
    C)   #77
    D)   #88

7) Who is the only Husky to score 2,000 or more points in a three-year career?

    A)   Ben Gordon
    B)   Ray Allen
    C)   Richard Hamilton
    D)   Emeka Okafor

8) In the UConn fight song, "U – Conn" a symbol of what?

    A)   Might
    B)   Pride
    C)   Power
    D)   Victory

9) How many career double-doubles did Emeka Okafor have in Big East competition?

   A) 21
   B) 24
   C) 27
   D) 30

10) Which All-American Team did Hasheem Thabeet make in a consensus basis in 2009?

   A) First Team
   B) Second Team
   C) Third Team
   D) None of the above

11) Who holds UConn's record for most steals in a career?

   A) Scott Burrell
   B) Doron Sheffer
   C) Khalid El-Amin
   D) Chris Smith

12) Since 1986-87, who holds UConn's single-game freshman scoring record?

   A) Khalid El-Amin
   B) Caron Butler
   C) Ray Allen
   D) Richard Hamilton

13) Who coached the Huskies immediately prior to Jim Calhoun?

   A) Dominic Perno
   B) Burr Carlson
   C) Donald Rowe
   D) Fred Shabel

14) Has UConn ever had a player drafted No. 1 overall in the NBA Draft?

   A) Yes
   B) No

15) What is UConn's largest-ever margin of victory over Seton Hall?

   A) 39 points
   B) 42 points
   C) 45 points
   D) 48 points

16) From what country is UConn's Charles Okwandu?

   A) Algeria
   B) Morocco
   C) Nigeria
   D) Tanzania

17) UConn's head coach Jim Calhoun is one of how many active NCAA Division 1 coaches with 800 or more career wins?

A) 2
B) 3
C) 4
D) 5

18) Which team ended UConn's thirty-three game winning streak at XL Center in 1996-97?

A) Memphis
B) Kentucky
C) North Carolina
D) Kansas

19) What was the official attendance at the 2009 Final Four match-up between UConn and Michigan State?

A) 62,456
B) 72,456
C) 82,456
D) 92,456

20) Who was UConn's first-ever official basketball coach?

A) John Donahue
B) Roy Guyer
C) J.W. Tasker
D) M.R. Swartz

21) Against which team was the Huskies' last regular-season conference loss in 2008-09?

   A) Syracuse
   B) Georgetown
   C) Pittsburgh
   D) Notre Dame

22) Did Wes Bialosuknia reach 1,000 career points at UConn in fewer games than Richard Hamilton?

   A) Yes
   B) No

23) How many years in the program's history has UConn made the NCAA Tournament?

   A) 24
   B) 26
   C) 29
   D) 30

24) What is UConn's all-time record for fewest points scored in a Big East game?

   A) 42
   B) 48
   C) 52
   D) 58

25) How many players on UConn's All-Century Basketball Team were originally from Connecticut?

    A) 6
    B) 8
    C) 9
    D) 11

26) What does UConn's home blue away jersey have written on the chest?

    A) Huskies
    B) UConn
    C) Connecticut
    D) "C" Logo

27) What is the Huskies' record for most consecutive Big East Tournament Championships?

    A) 2
    B) 3
    C) 4
    D) 5

28) Who was the first-ever African-American player to sign with UConn?

    A) Alan T. Busby
    B) Harrison Fitch Sr.
    C) Earl Wilson
    D) Tony Hanson

29) What is UConn's record for most consecutive wins to start a season?

    A) 16 games
    B) 17 games
    C) 19 games
    D) 20 games

30) Hawley Armory was first used for UConn basketball in 1914-15?

    A) Yes
    B) No

31) Who scored UConn's first points in the 2009 NCAA Tournament?

    A) Jeff Adrien
    B) Hasheem Thabeet
    C) A.J. Price
    D) Robinson Stanley

32) What is the Huskies' record for most points scored in one half?

    A) 63
    B) 68
    C) 73
    D) 78

33) How many times has UConn been beaten while ranked No. 1 in the AP Poll?

    A) 3
    B) 4
    C) 5
    D) 6

34) In which of these categories did UConn lead the nation in 2003-04 and 2004-05?

    A) Rebounding
    B) Scoring Defense
    C) Steals
    D) Assists

35) What are the most consecutive Big East Tournament Championship games UConn has lost?

    A) 0
    B) 1
    C) 2
    D) 3

36) How many UConn head coaches lasted one season or less?

    A) 1
    B) 2
    C) 5
    D) 6

37) Which season did UConn lead the nation in free-throw percentage?

    A) 1945-46
    B) 1959-60
    C) 1976-77
    D) 1980-81

38) Which team gave UConn its first-ever home loss at Gampel Pavilion?

    A) St. John's
    B) Villanova
    C) North Carolina State
    D) Georgetown

39) Which Big East school has the highest all-time winning percentage against the Huskies?

    A) St. John's
    B) Georgetown
    C) Pittsburgh
    D) Syracuse

40) What is UConn's record for most losses in one season at XL Center?

    A) 6
    B) 7
    C) 10
    D) 11

41) What is UConn's record for most consecutive NCAA Tournament wins?

  A) 5
  B) 6
  C) 7
  D) 8

42) Who was the first-ever Husky to appear on the cover of *Sports Illustrated*?

  A) Ricky Moore
  B) Khalid El-Amin
  C) Hasheem Thabeet
  D) Emeka Okafor

43) What is the name of the UConn tradition that takes place in Gampel Pavilion the night before the first official practice of the season?

  A) Midnight Practice
  B) Fans Night
  C) Night Practice
  D) First Night

44) UConn's new scoreboards and video board displays in Gampel Pavilion replace units installed in what year?

  A) 1990
  B) 2000
  C) 2005
  D) No new boards are being installed

45) How many total seasons of college basketball has UConn's Jim Calhoun coached?

    A) 33
    B) 35
    C) 37
    D) 39

46) Clifford Robinson was the first UConn player to wear what jersey number?

    A) 00
    B) 6
    C) 7
    D) 26

47) When was the most recent season UConn led the nation in scoring margin?

    A) 1950-51
    B) 1954-55
    C) 1960-61
    D) 1964-65

48) How many players are in the UConn Huskies of Honor?

    A) 13
    B) 15
    C) 17
    D) 19

49) In 2008-09, against which team did A.J. Price score a season high 36 points?

    A) Syracuse
    B) Marquette
    C) Providence
    D) Texas A&M

50) Which Husky played the most career Big East games?

    A) Eric Haywood
    B) Donny Marshall
    C) Brian Fair
    D) Kevin Freeman

How many times have you been on the cover of *Sports Illustrated*? Let's face it, appearing on it once is something to brag about. Now try telling friends and family that *SI* featured you three times within five months. That is precisely the story Emeka Okafor was telling them after his third appearance on an *SI* cover on April 14, 2004. His story began when he appeared on the Nov. 24, 2003 College Basketball – Preview 2003-04 edition along with Lady Husky Diana Taurasi. Weeks later on April 12, 2004 he appeared as an NCAA National Champion after earning the Most Outstanding Player of the Final Four award. *Sports Illustrated* then released a "Special Double Commemorative" edition to honor the UConn men's and women's basketball programs' national championship runs, for which Okafor was once again chosen for the cover.

Huskyology Trivia Challenge

1) C – 9 (1990, 1995, 1996, 1998-2000, and 2002-04)

2) A – Donyell Marshall (He hit 20 of 20 FTs verses St. John's on Jan. 15, 1994 [UConn 85, St. John's 81].)

3) D – 1989-90 (James Calhoun led the Huskies to a 31-6 [.838] record that season.)

4) B – No (With 44 steals in the season, Jerome Dyson set the team's high-water mark.)

5) C – Ray Allen (From 1994-96 Allen set the team's record for most consecutive games scoring in double figures.)

6) A – #55 (Several players have worn #55 in their UConn careers. The most recent was Kyle Bailey in 2008-09. NCAA rules do not allow numbers higher than five on a jersey.)

7) C – Richard Hamilton (Hamilton scored 2,036 career points in three seasons from 1996-99.)

8) A – Might (The lyrics go: "U – Conn Husky, symbol of might to the foe…")

9) B – 24 (2002-04)

10) B – Second Team (Hasheem was a Consensus Second Team All-American as selected by the AP, USBWA, and *The Sporting News*.)

11) A – Scott Burrell (From 1990-93 Burrell had 310 steals.)

12) D – Richard Hamilton (Hamilton scored 31 points on two occasions his freshman season. The first was on Feb. 25, 1997, versus Pittsburgh and the second was on March 21, 1997, versus Nebraska.)

13) A – Dominic Perno (He led the Huskies from 1977-86.)

14) B – No (UConn's highest all-time selections are
Hasheem Thabeet #2 overall in 2009 to the
Memphis Grizzlies and Emeka Okafor #2 overall in
2004 to the Charlotte Bobcats.)

15) B – 42 points (Seton Hall, 99-57 on Feb. 11, 2006)

16) C – Nigeria (Okwandu was born in Lagos, Nigeria and
is a 2004 graduate of King's High School.)

17) A – 2 (Only Duke's Mike Krzyzewski [833] and UConn's
Jim Calhoun [805] currently have greater than 800
career wins.)

18) D – Kansas (Kansas's 73-65 victory over UConn ended
the streak on Jan. 19, 1997.)

19) B – 72,456 (Ford Field; Detroit, Michigan)

20) A – John Donahue (Coach Donahue was named the
team's first official coach in 1915. He led the team
for four seasons earning an 11-23 [.324] record.)

21) C – Pittsburgh (The Panthers took advantage of an
home-court advantage in defeating the Huskies
70-60 on March 7, 2009.)

22) A – Yes (Wes reached the 1,000-point milestone in a
mere 47 games compared to Richard's 55 games.)

23) C – 29 (From the school's first appearance in 1950-51
through 2008-09 UConn has played in 29 NCAA
Tournaments, including 1996.)

24) A – 42 (On Feb. 27, 1982, the Huskies could only
manage 42 points in a 42-60 loss versus
Georgetown.)

25) B – 8 (Scott Burrell, Walt Dropo, Tony Hanson, Earl Kelley, Art Quimby, Chris Smith, Corny Thompson, and Vin Yokabaskas all hail from Connecticut.)

26) C – Connecticut (Blue away jerseys have Connecticut in white letters, whereas the Huskies white home jerseys have UConn in blue with red outline around the U.)

27) A – 2 (1998 and 1999)

28) B – Harrison Fitch Sr. (His freshman year was in 1932.)

29) C – 19 games (UConn began the 1998-99 season with a 19-game winning streak. Syracuse ended the streak with a 59-42 victory on Feb. 1, 1999.)

30) A – Yes (The final two games of the 1914-15 season were played in the newly completed Hawley Armory.)

31) D – Robinson Stanley (At 18:37 Stanley hit a jumper to tie the game at 2 points each vs. Chattanooga in the first round of the 2009 NCAA Tournament.)

32) B – 68 (UConn scored 68 points in a single half on two separate occasions, once versus Hartford on Dec. 29, 1996 and once versus AIC on Dec. 23, 1957.)

33) C – 5 (The most recent occurrence was in 2008-09 when Pitt defeated UConn 76-68 on Feb. 16, 2009. Pitt took over the No. 1 ranking in the next week's poll.)

34) A – Rebounding (2003-04 [9.7% margin] and 2004-05 [11.3% margin])

35) B – 1 (UConn has never lost 2 games or more in a row in the tournament.)

36) C – 5 (J.W. Tasker [1921-22], Roy Guyer [1922-23], J.O. Christian [Interim 1935-36], Blair Gullion [1945-46], and George Wigton [Interim 1963])

37) D – 1980-81 (As a team the Huskies hit 487 of 623 free throws [78.2%] that season.)

38) A – St. John's (UConn's first-ever loss in Gampel Pavilion took place on Jan. 12, 1991. St. John's stole a 72-59 victory that night.)

39) D – Syracuse (The Orangemen's 47-36 all-time record versus UConn gives them a .566 winning percentage.)

40) B – 7 (In 1986-87 UConn was 2-7 [.222] at XL Center.)

41) C – 7 (UConn had two stretches of seven-game winning streaks in the NCAA Tournament. The 1st included 6 games in 1999 then the 1st game of 2000. The 2nd included 6 games in 2004 then the 1st game of 2005.)

42) A – Ricky Moore (Moore was featured on the cover of the April 5, 1999 issue aptly titled "Yes, UConn".)

43) D – First Night (Fans are welcomed to Gampel to interact with players and coaches, to watch highlight videos, and to watch both the men's and women's team participate in separate scrimmages.)

44) B – 2000 (The new scoreboard is approximately 12.5 feet by 23 feet, which is more than twice the size of the scoreboard installed in 2000.)

45) C – 37 (Coach Calhoun completed his 37th season as a head basketball coach in 2008-09. He began his collegiate head coaching career in 1972 at Northeastern University.)

46) A – 00 (Robinson is the only Husky to ever don the 00. He wore the number from 1986-89.)

47) D – 1964-65 (This is the only season the Huskies led the league in scoring margin. Their scoring margin that season was 18.6.)

48) A – 13 (Ray Allen [1993-96], Wes Bialosuknia [1964-67], Walt Dropo [1942-47], Richard Hamilton [1996-99], Tony Hanson [1973-77], Toby Kimball [1961-65], Donyell Marshall [1991-94], Emeka Okafor [2001-04], Art Quimby [1951-55], Clifford Robinson [1985-89], Chris Smith [1988-92], Corny Thompson [1978-82], and Vin Yokabaskas [1948-52])

49) B – Marquette (Price's 36 points were the most points any Husky scored in a single game in 2008-09.)

50) C – Brian Fair (From 1992-95 Fair played in 72 Big East games.)

Note: All answers valid as of the end of the 2008-09 season, unless otherwise indicated in the question itself.

1) What was UConn's all-time record at Storrs Field House?

Answers begin on page 75

   A) 282-85
   B) 382-85
   C) 482-85
   D) None of the above

2) How many times have the Huskies played in front of a crowed of 30,000 or more?

   A) 12
   B) 14
   C) 16
   D) 18

3) UConn was one of seven teams ranked No. 1 in the AP Poll in the 2008-09 season.

   A) True
   B) False

4) What was UConn seeded in the 2008 NCAA Tournament?

   A) #1
   B) #2
   C) #3
   D) #4

5) Who was UConn's first-ever Big East opponent?

   A) Seton Hall
   B) Georgetown
   C) St. John's
   D) Boston College

6) What is UConn's largest-ever margin of victory over Cincinnati?

   A) 30 points
   B) 35 points
   C) 40 points
   D) 45 points

7) When was the last time Yale defeated UConn?

   A) 1981-82
   B) 1986-87
   C) 1993-94
   D) 2001-02

8) Who holds the Huskies' record for most points scored in a freshman season?

   A) Richard Hamilton
   B) Earl Kelley
   C) Corny Thompson
   D) Jerome Dyson

9) Did UConn attempt more free throws than its opponents in the 2008-09 season?

   A) Yes
   B) No

10) What is the Huskies' record for most team rebounds in a single game?

   A) 66
   B) 71
   C) 76
   D) 81

11) Which of the following UConn players never scored 30 or more points in a single NCAA Tournament game?

   A) Ray Allen
   B) Ben Gordon
   C) Rashad Anderson
   D) Caron Butler

12) What was UConn known as when it played its first-ever basketball game versus Windham High School in 1901?

   A) Connecticut Agricultural College
   B) Connecticut A&M
   C) Connecticut College
   D) Connecticut Farm Tech

13) In which category did UConn lead the nation in 1957?

   A)   Field-Goal Percentage
   B)   Free-Throw Percentage
   C)   Scoring Defense
   D)   Scoring Offense

14) When was the last time a No. 1-ranked UConn team lost to an unranked opponent?

   A)   2001
   B)   2003
   C)   2004
   D)   2006

15) What is UConn's all-time record for most victories in a season?

   A)   31
   B)   32
   C)   33
   D)   34

16) Against which team did UConn's Jim Calhoun get his 500th all-time career win?

   A)   Marquette
   B)   Georgetown
   C)   Boston College
   D)   Miami

17) In 2008-09,did any UConn player have five or more steals in a single game?

   A) Yes
   B) No

18) All time, how many total weeks has UConn held the No. 1 ranking in the AP Poll?

   A) 20
   B) 24
   C) 28
   D) 32

19) When was the most recent season UConn scored over 3,000 points as a team?

   A) 2003-04
   B) 2005-06
   C) 2006-07
   D) 2007-08

20) What is the Huskies' record for most consecutive NCAA Tournament losses?

   A) 4
   B) 7
   C) 11
   D) 14

21) What is the combined winning percentage of UConn head coaches who lasted one season or less?

    A) .587
    B) .687
    C) .787
    D) .887

22) What was UConn's total attendance (home, away, and neutral) for the 2008-09 season?

    A) 391,852
    B) 427,773
    C) 495,997
    D) 500,741

23) Where did Hugh Greer coach before UConn?

    A) Fairfield
    B) Hartford
    C) Quinnipiac
    D) None of the above

24) What is UConn's all-time record versus the North Carolina Tar Heels?

    A) 0-6
    B) 1-5
    C) 3-3
    D) 5-1

25) When was UConn's team record for most points scored in a season set?

    A) 1989-90
    B) 1993-94
    C) 1998-99
    D) 2003-04

26) Including postseason play, has UConn surpassed the all-time 1,500-win mark?

    A) Yes
    B) No

27) How many times has UConn been a No.-1 seed in the NCAA Tournament?

    A) 3
    B) 4
    C) 5
    D) 6

28) Which one-season UConn head coach had the best winning percentage?

    A) George Wigton
    B) J.W. Tasker
    C) Roy Tasker
    D) Blair Gullion

29) Which decade did UConn have its lowest winning percentage?

    A) 1910s
    B) 1920s
    C) 1930s
    D) 1940s

30) How many times in school history has UConn won 30 or more games in a season (including postseason)?

    A) 7
    B) 8
    C) 9
    D) 10

31) How many Huskies have scored 1,000+ career points?

    A) 40
    B) 43
    C) 46
    D) 49

32) How many total team turnovers did UConn have in the 2008-09 season?

    A) 329
    B) 365
    C) 412
    D) 458

33) What is UConn's all-time record for largest margin of victory in an NCAA Tournament game?

    A) 25 points
    B) 29 points
    C) 56 points
    D) 62 points

34) Which Husky had the highest three-point percentage in 2008-09 (minimum 25 attempts)?

    A) Jeff Adrien
    B) Jerome Dyson
    C) Craig Austrie
    D) A.J. Price

35) When was the first and only season the Huskies made more than 50% of their shots from the field?

    A) 1978-79
    B) 1980-81
    C) 1998-99
    D) 2003-04

36) Has UConn ever had four players selected in the first round of the NBA Draft in the same year?

    A) Yes
    B) No

37) Who was the most recent player to lead UConn in scoring for three seasons?

A) Caron Butler
B) Ben Gordon
C) Richard Hamilton
D) Chris Smith

38) Each of UConn's National Championship teams also won the Big East regular season and conference tournament.

A) True
B) False

39) How many coaches and administrators are in the University of Connecticut Men's Basketball Huskies of Honor?

A) 1
B) 2
C) 3
D) 4

40) In the decade of the 1950s, did UConn have a winning record every season?

A) Yes
B) No

41) How many Huskies averaged 20 or more minutes of playing time per game in the 2008-09 season?

    A) 7
    B) 8
    C) 9
    D) 10

42) Who was the most recent Husky named CoSIDA Academic All-American?

    A) Randy Lavigne
    B) Hasheem Thabeet
    C) Emeka Okafor
    D) Khalid El-Amin

43) Which of the following players did not score over 2,000 career points while at UConn?

    A) Tony Hanson
    B) Richard Hamilton
    C) Chris Smith
    D) All of them scored over 2,000

44) What is UConn's longest winning streak in Gampel Pavilion?

    A) 15 games
    B) 16 games
    C) 20 games
    D) 21 games

45) How many Huskies have been awarded Big East Defensive Player of the Year?

    A) 5
    B) 6
    C) 7
    D) 8

46) Where did UConn head coach Jim Calhoun play college basketball?

    A) Boston College
    B) Wellesley
    C) American International
    D) Emerson

47) Does UConn have a losing record against Duke?

    A) Yes
    B) No

48) Which school has beaten UConn more than once at the XL Center?

    A) Louisville
    B) Notre Dame
    C) Rhode Island
    D) West Virginia

49) How many NIT Championships has UConn won?

    A) 0
    B) 1
    C) 2
    D) 3

50) How many seasons was UConn a member of the Yankee Conference?

    A) 28
    B) 29
    C) 30
    D) 31

Home court advantage should be more than just a fanciful notion. In 1989-90 UConn celebrated the inaugural season at the newly constructed Gampel Pavilion in Storrs, Conn. Unlike most house-warming parties however, UConn decided not to be gracious hosts to its house guests. Visiting teams including St. John's, Fairfield, Boston College, Providence, and Seton Hall, won a collective zero games at Gampel that season. In fact, it would not be until the fifth game of the following season that UConn would finally lose at their new home. All told, UConn has enjoyed nine undefeated seasons in Gampel since it opened. That is a decided home court advantage in an extremely competitive conference and league.

1) A – 282-85 (This gave them a .768 all-time winning percentage at Storrs Field House.)

2) C – 16 (From 72,456 fans on April 4, 2009 in Detroit to 30,136 fans on Jan. 19, 1985 in Syracuse)

3) B – False (Only six teams shared the No. 1 ranking: North Carolina, Pittsburgh, Wake Forest, Duke, UConn, and Louisville in 2008-09.)

4) D – #4 (UConn was the #4 seed in the West Regional.)

5) A – Seton Hall (The Huskies played their first-ever Big East regular-season game versus Seton Hall on Dec. 22, 1979. UConn won 89-73 at home.)

6) D – 45 points (On March 9, 2008, UConn crushed Cincinnati 96-51.)

7) B – 1986-87 (Yale has not enjoyed a victory over UConn since Dec. 2, 1986. It took an overtime period for Yale to grab a 77-75 victory.)

8) C – Corny Thompson (In 1978-79 Thompson scored a team-leading 538 points [18.6 per game] to set UConn's freshman scoring record.)

9) A – Yes (UConn made 662 of 976 [.678] free throws versus 320 of 458 [.699] by their opponents.)

10) D – 81 (UConn players corralled 81 boards on Feb. 27, 1965, vs. New Hampshire [UConn 109, NH 61].)

11) C – Rashad Anderson (Rashad's NCAA Tournament game high was 28 points versus Alabama on March 27, 2004 [UConn 87, Alabama 71].)

12) A – Connecticut Agricultural College (Basketball would not earn varsity sport status at CAC until 1903.)

13) D – Scoring Offense (UConn scored 2,183 points in 25 games [87.3 ave.] to lead the league in 1956-57.)

14) B – 2003 (On Nov. 26, 2003, an unranked Georgia Tech got a 77-61 victory over UConn in New York.)

15) C – 34 (In 1998-99 the Huskies were 34-2.)

16) C – Boston College (Coach Calhoun earned his 500th career victory on Jan. 11, 1998, at Boston College with an 80-68 over the Eagles.)

17) B – No (Three players had four steals in a game: Kemba Walker [Wisconsin on Nov. 24, 2008], Jerome Dyson [Georgetown on Dec. 29, 2008], and Craig Austrie [Chattanooga on March 19, 2009].)

18) C – 28 (Includes AP No. 1 rankings from 1995-2009.)

19) A – 2003-04 (UConn had 3,073 points that season.)

20) B – 7 (From March 16, 1956 through March 11, 1963, UConn lost seven-straight NCAA Tournament games.)

21) A – .587 (These five coaches combined for an average winning percentage of .587.)

22) C – 495,997 (Home [200,284], Away [118,181], and Neutral [177,532])

23) D – None of the above (Coach Greer's coaching career started and ended at UConn [1946-63].)

24) B – 1-5 (UConn's only win in the series came at Gampel Pavilion on Jan. 19, 2002, [UConn 86, North Carolina 54] in front of 10,027 fans.)

25) A – 2003-04 (UConn's team total 3,073 points that season are the most in team history.)

26) B – No (As of the end of the 2008-09 season, UConn is one win away from the 1,500 wins milestone.)

27) C – 5 (1990, 1996, 1999, 2006, and 2009)

28) B – J.W. Tasker (J.W. Tasker [.750], Roy Guyer [.571], J.O. Christian [.231], Blair Gullion [.652], and George Wigton [.733])

29) A – 1910s (UConn's 26-40 record gave them their all-time lowest winning percentage in a single decade.)

30) A – 7 (1989-99 [31-6], 1995-96 [30-2], 1997-98 [32-5], 1998-99 [34-2], 2003-04 [33-6], 2005-06 [30-4], and 2008-09 [31-5])

31) B – 43 (The most recent players to join the 1,000 point club at UConn are A.J. Price [1,284], Jerome Dyson [1,044], and Hasheem Thabeet [1,028] in 2008-09.)

32) D – 458 (A.J. Price had the most turnovers [94].)

33) C – 56 points (UConn's 103-47 victory over Chattanooga in the 2009 tournament set the team's new record for largest margin of victory.)

34) D – A.J. Price (Price hit 82 of 204 three-point attempts for a .402 percentage in 2008-09.)

35) B – 1980-81 (As a team the Huskies knocked down 765-1,483 shots [51.6%] that season.)

36) A – Yes (Rudy Gray [Houston Rockets], Hilton Armstrong [New Orleans/Oklahoma City Hornets], Marcus Williams [New Jersey Nets], and Josh Boone [New Jersey Nets] were all drafted in the first round of the 2006 draft. Only Duke and North Carolina had previously had four players taken in the first round in the same year.)

37) C – Richard Hamilton (Hamilton led all Husky scorers for three seasons: 1996-97 [15.9 ppg], 1997-98 [21.5 ppg], and 1998-99 [21.5 ppg].)

38) B – False (Although UConn won the Big East Regular Season, Big East Tournament, and NCAA Championship in 1999, they failed to win all 3 in 2004, missing the conference regular season title.)

39) D – 4 (Jim Calhoun [head coach], Hugh Greer [head coach], Dee Rowe [head coach], and John Toner [Athletic Director])

40) A – Yes (Ranging from their highest, .885 to their lowest, .607 through the decade)

41) A – 7 (Price [31.8], Adrien [34.6], Thabeet [31.8], Dyson [29.3], Walker [25.2], Robinson [24.9], and Austrie [25.3])

42) C – Emeka Okafor (Not only was Emeka named a CoSIDA Academic All-American in 2003-04, but he was the CoSIDA Academic All-American of the Year, graduating with a degree in finance in 3 years, with a 3.75 GPA.)

43) A – Tony Hanson (Hanson missed the 2,000 point milestone by 10 points, with 1,990 career points.)

44) B – 16 games (UConn won every game played in Gampel Pavilion in 2007-08 [8] and 2008-09 [8]. They also won 16 straight at Gampel from 1996-97 through 1997-98.)

45) A – 5 (Five players have won the award seven times. Most recently, Hasheem Thabeet for his defensive play in 2007-08 and 2008-09.)

46) C – American International (From 1965-68 Calhoun played for AIC helping them to make the Division II playoffs his senior year.)

47) B – No (UConn and Duke are evenly matched at 4-4 all-time in series play. The Huskies won the first four meetings, with their last victory in 1991.)

48) C – Rhode Island (Rhode Island [3-2], Louisville [1-1], Notre Dame [6-1], and West Virginia [2-0])

49) B – 1 (In 1987-88 UConn beat Ohio State in the NIT Championship game to earn its first Postseason NIT Championship [UConn 72, Ohio State 67].)

50) A – 28 (UConn played its first game in the Yankee Conference in 1948-49 and its last in 1975-76.)

Note: All answers valid as of the end of the 2008-09 season, unless otherwise indicated in the question itself.

1) Who is popularly considered the "Father of UConn Basketball"?

Answers begin on page 83

    A)   Sumner Dole
    B)   M.R. Swartz
    C)   John Donahue
    D)   Donald Rowe

2) From 1939-68 UConn defeated what team 24 consecutive times at home?

    A)   Coast Guard
    B)   Rhode Island
    C)   New Hampshire
    D)   St. John's

3) How many times has UConn's Jim Calhoun's alma mater, American International, defeated UConn?

    A)   0
    B)   5
    C)   10
    D)   15

4) Did Coach Calhoun win his first-ever Big East Conference game as head coach of UConn?

    A)   Yes
    B)   No

5) How many times since 1948-49 has UConn's leading scorer averaged less than 10 points per game?

A) 1
B) 2
C) 3
D) 4

6) What was UConn's nickname from 1901-33?

A) Huskies
B) UConners
C) Statesmen
D) Aggies

7) Which player holds UConn's record for most points scored in an NCAA Championship game?

A) Richard Hamilton
B) Ben Gordon
C) Khalid El-Amin
D) Rashad Anderson

8) How many UConn players have been drafted in the first round of the NBA Draft?

A) 13
B) 14
C) 15
D) 16

9) What were UConn's originally chosen school colors?

A) Yellow
B) Green
C) Red
D) Blue

10) Did UConn lead at the half in both of its NCAA Championship games?

A) Yes
B) No

1) D – Donald Rowe ("Dee" Rowe became Huskies head coach in 1969. He's also acted as Special Advisor for Athletics to the university.)

2) C – New Hampshire (This is the third longest such streak in NCAA basketball history.)

3) A – 0 (UConn is 20-0 versus American International.)

4) B – No (Coach Calhoun lost his first Big East game played on Dec. 13, 1986 [UConn 51, Villanova 66].)

5) A – 1 (In 1948-49 Pete Lind averaged 9.7 PPG to lead all Husky scorers.)

6) D – Aggies (The name came from the school's agricultural heritage.)

7) A – Richard Hamilton (Hamilton scored 27 points versus Duke in the 1999 NCAA Championship game.)

8) C – 15 (Ranging from Tate George in 1990 to Hasheem Thabeet in 2009)

9) D – Blue (White was added later. It was said to distinguish UConn's colors from Yale's.)

10) B – No (At the half UConn led 41-26 versus Georgia Tech in 2004, but trailed 37-39 versus Duke in 1999.)

Note: All answers valid as of the end of the 2008-09 season, unless otherwise indicated in the question itself.

Player / Team Score Sheet

Name:_____

Preseason			Regular Season			Conference Tournament			Championship Game			Overtime Bonus	
1		26	1		26	1		26	1		26	1	
2		27	2		27	2		27	2		27	2	
3		28	3		28	3		28	3		28	3	
4		29	4		29	4		29	4		29	4	
5		30	5		30	5		30	5		30	5	
6		31	6		31	6		31	6		31	6	
7		32	7		32	7		32	7		32	7	
8		33	8		33	8		33	8		33	8	
9		34	9		34	9		34	9		34	9	
10		35	10		35	10		35	10		35	10	
11		36	11		36	11		36	11		36		
12		37	12		37	12		37	12		37		
13		38	13		38	13		38	13		38		
14		39	14		39	14		39	14		39		
15		40	15		40	15		40	15		40		
16		41	16		41	16		41	16		41		
17		42	17		42	17		42	17		42		
18		43	18		43	18		43	18		43		
19		44	19		44	19		44	19		44		
20		45	20		45	20		45	20		45		
21		46	21		46	21		46	21		46		
22		47	22		47	22		47	22		47		
23		48	23		48	23		48	23		48		
24		49	24		49	24		49	24		49		
25		50	25		50	25		50	25		50		
___ x 1 =___			___ x 2 =___			___ x 3 =___			___ x 4 =___			___ x 4 =___	

Multiply total number correct by point value/quarter to calculate totals for each quarter.

Add total of all quarters below.

Total Points:_____

Thank you for playing *Huskyology Trivia Challenge*.

Additional score sheets are available at:
www.TriviaGameBooks.com

Player / Team Score Sheet

Name:_____

Preseason		Regular Season		Conference Tournament		Championship Game		Overtime Bonus	
1	26	1	26	1	26	1	26	1	
2	27	2	27	2	27	2	27	2	
3	28	3	28	3	28	3	28	3	
4	29	4	29	4	29	4	29	4	
5	30	5	30	5	30	5	30	5	
6	31	6	31	6	31	6	31	6	
7	32	7	32	7	32	7	32	7	
8	33	8	33	8	33	8	33	8	
9	34	9	34	9	34	9	34	9	
10	35	10	35	10	35	10	35	10	
11	36	11	36	11	36	11	36		
12	37	12	37	12	37	12	37		
13	38	13	38	13	38	13	38		
14	39	14	39	14	39	14	39		
15	40	15	40	15	40	15	40		
16	41	16	41	16	41	16	41		
17	42	17	42	17	42	17	42		
18	43	18	43	18	43	18	43		
19	44	19	44	19	44	19	44		
20	45	20	45	20	45	20	45		
21	46	21	46	21	46	21	46		
22	47	22	47	22	47	22	47		
23	48	23	48	23	48	23	48		
24	49	24	49	24	49	24	49		
25	50	25	50	25	50	25	50		
___ x 1 =___		___ x 2 =___		___ x 3 =___		___ x 4 =___		___ x 4 =___	

Multiply total number correct by point value/quarter to calculate totals for each quarter.

Add total of all quarters below.

Total Points:_____

Thank you for playing *Huskyology Trivia Challenge*.

Additional score sheets are available at:
www.TriviaGameBooks.com